D1523670

ALSO BY JULIA HARTWIG

Pożegnania (*Farewells*, 1956)

Wolne ręce (*Free Hands*, 1969)

Dwoistość (*Doubleness*, 1971)

Czuwanie (*Vigil*, 1978)

Chwila postoju (*Brief Stopover*, 1980)

Dziennik amerykański (*American Journal*, 1980)

Obcowanie (*Communing*, 1987)

Czułość (*Tenderness*, 1992)

Zobaczone (*Seen*, 1999)

Błyski (*Flashes*, 2001)

Nie ma odpowiedzi (*There Is No Answer*, 2001)

Wiersze amerykańskie (*American Poems*, 2002)

Mowiąc nie tylko do siebie (*Speaking Not Only to Myself*, 2003)

Bez pożegnania (*No Farewells*, 2004)

In Praise of the Unfinished

In Praise of the
Unfinished

— Selected Poems —

Julia Hartwig

TRANSLATED BY
JOHN AND BOGDANA CARPENTER

Alfred A. Knopf   New York   2008

THIS IS A BORZOI BOOK
PUBLISHED BY ALFRED A. KNOPF

www.aaknopf.com

Library of Congress Cataloging-in-Publication Data

Hartwig, Julia.
[Poems. English. Selections]
In praise of the unfinished : selected poems / Julia Hartwig: translated
by John and Bogdana Carpenter.
p.   cm.
ISBN 978-0-307-26720-7
1. Hartwig, Julia—Translations into English. I. Carpenter, John,
1936– II. Carpenter, Bogdana. III. Title.
PG7167.A75A2 2008
891.8'517—dc22
2007042194

Manufactured in the United States of America
First Edition

CONTENTS

Fortune-Telling from the Seabed

When the sea bay grows quiet, it is as if the whole world has calmed down.

Transparent water reveals the clear constellations of pebbles resting on the bottom.

And the absurd hope awakens that everything scattered chaotically in the world will settle down again, in a natural order.

Return to My Childhood Home

Amid a dark silence of pines—the shouts of young birches calling each other.

Everything is as it was. Nothing is as it was.

Speak to me, Lord of the child. Speak, innocent terror!

To understand nothing. Each time in a different way, from the first cry to the last breath.

Yet happy moments come to me from the past, like bridesmaids carrying oil lamps.

Philemon and Baucis

One of them gets up at night. In a nightshirt she shuffles blindly to the kitchen to get some water. The other listens.

This shuffling bothers him, he is awake, irritated, he mutters impatiently.

Suddenly his hair stands on end.

Is this shuffling real, or is it only a memory, in the past, in nonexistence?

It is real! She really shuffles. So, they are still together. Grateful and reconciled, he falls back into his fragile sleep.

I Will Perform This Miracle for You

dedicated to H.

They love her so much that they hate the old age growing in her. Tall and handsome they walk by her side, and look at her with the eyes of their childhood.

Until now they hear her voice ringing in their ears like an Easter bell swinging in the friendly wind. It always accompanied her quick movements, carrying objects toward her.

So when she trips in the street, they hiss: Grandma, don't pretend!

And when she hunches over, they call: Grandma, straighten up!

Hearing it, a stranger would consider them cruel.

But once more she makes the effort, straightens up, her face flooded by the light of love.

Is That All?

What is a poem worth if it doesn't perform a miracle?

A mother is resurrected and once again strokes our heads.

We forget our own death, and our legs never hurt.

No one talks too much. Moralizing ends, as well as boasting. Everyone lives according to his measure. Dressing and cleaning don't devour time.

Children are not caricatures of their parents, and parents, always young, leave one day for a walk before sunset.

So is that all you expect from a miracle?

Old Fashions

I remember an old, meticulously executed print.

Swallowed by a whale, a small man with a frock coat sits inside its belly at a table, lit by an oil lamp.

But from time to time the whale gets hungry. And here is the second print.

A powerful wave of seawater rushes with a shoal of small fish through the throat to the belly.

The table with the lamp is knocked down. The small man, diving, nestles against the slick wall inside the whale's massive bulk.

After the wave retreats he sets up his table again, hangs the lamp, and begins to work.

Is he studying the Old Testament? Is he studying maps?

What else could be of interest to a traveler miraculously saved from a shipwreck?

I often think of this print as I lay books down on my table for work, after tightly closing windows and doors.

Evergreen

Stay forever green tree of joyful existence
tree rooted in the sky
and tree drawing its sap from the earth
tree of illusion and tree of dream
solitary tree and tree seeking support among other trees
rooted tree and tree eager to travel
tree frightened by night and tree finding shelter in the night
talkative tree and tree fond of silence
tree slender as a cemetery obelisk and tree spread out like a family
tree with a sharp outline
and tree unable to cope with its own shape
ecstatic tree entirely devoted to matters of clouds
and tree curiously peeking into windows of households
tree of eternal torment and tree of soothing gentleness
sacrificial tree tree eternally green
Evergreen

You are always present within me
elegant tree and poor tree
tree bent over an orphanage of shrubs
tree looking at itself in the moon
and dripping with sweat in the sun's heat
a tree white from rain and a thirsty tree
tree gracefully open to every passerby

and a proud tree hiding foreign deities
tree of pleasure of nostalgia of torment
tree eternally green
Evergreen

Tree that is the tower of our desires
abode of birds and angels
my eyes my arms my force
surrendered to your force
so that you last in us eternally green
Evergreen

Tree of indomitable growth
and wounded tree
torn tree and burnt-out tree
tree where the fearful heart of a squirrel beats
and tree greeting the storm with a beating of drums
to measure its strength against the sparkling glance
faithful tree and tree full of betrayal
tree of endless incarnations yet always reborn
stay with us and teach us endurance
royal from childhood on
eternally green
and eternally alive
Evergreen

Tenderness

She looks at you craning her neck
You are her heaven and on her sky
your face marks the sun and bad weather
she is a small chick that would like to sit in the branches of your arms
full of chirping and so dependent on you
it would move the heart even of a stone

So many years have gone by and in the mirror
where you look her image still appears
tiny standing next to you craning her neck
and a request or question already forgotten
which it is too late to answer today

My Greetings to a Distant River

If you look on this continent
for what has endured
what is permanent and eternal
consider the rivers and mountains
They remember more than people
their memory is more faithful and deeply hidden
they are neither talkative nor banal

Old Iowa River after many years I greet you again
where the colors of spring and autumn look at themselves
you who witnessed old-fashioned houses and settlements
give way to structures of glass and concrete
Old river you picked a sunny October for my return
so looking at you in your bed freely chosen in liberty
trees and shrubs running down to the banks
I could admire you lit up with a quiet glow
blue as a vein pulsing in a living body

Here on the earth through which you travel
not boasting of fertile richness
—what mother seeks praise for nursing her children—
you run natural and singing
along a province that took your name
to meet plain and rough-hewn people
tired from labor of the day that has ended
who fall asleep at table still clasping a mug

River you are an incarnation of grace
you are their dance though they dance rarely
your hum is their song you are their music teacher
when they unite their voices in church hymns
or meet over beer striking up familiar tunes

River I greet you who are an eternal return
make my return to you permanent
preserve my gaze and my entreaties in your current
when far away on another continent
I will remember you and the arms of my friends
open when I am in need

How to Honor a Place

An inscription announces that the continental divide
between the Pacific and the Atlantic
runs exactly here

A river with its beginning in this region
must think hard
which of the two oceans it should belong to
which mother it acknowledges
in whose gullet it is to be lost forever
and become nameless

How to honor this unique place
with a shout with silence
I am standing over the divide
as if on the back of a bison blinded by sun
with its legs spread out The rain of waters
flows on both its shining sides

And I
where do I belong

Translating American Poets

They might not care for such a change of place—
from Long Island Santa Barbara the City Lights bookstore in San
      Francisco
from a trapper's shack on a clear stream in Pate Valley
from beds where they lie still half asleep
from smoke-filled taverns and clubs
from motels where they throw off shoes after a day's hike in a clay
      valley
from a secluded farm in Missouri from a well-to-do house in
Washington
from a night bar in New York City—

They rebel against this uncalled-for move
to Eastern Europe which they know so little
though it's not you but your poems that have wandered over to us
You don't even know what a warm welcome met them here
for reasons I can only guess without certainty:
because you honored in them your anxieties and vanities
your maladies and follies your cars and flowers
your travels and landscapes gathered along the way
your hatred of big cities and rapture over them
Chicago New York New Orleans the Golden Gate Brooklyn Bridge
names dreamt for years by European teenagers
together with hopes for great change and fame

This is the dowry you bring

in poems not aiming at greatness but showing the calendar of
        ordinariness

seen through the eyes of a farmer a neurotic and hypochondriac

a dipsomaniac a nymphomaniac a tramp

brimming with life trampled by a gang of misfortunes and failures

proud of democracy and cursing its abuses

It is wonderful to be able to look at one's own country

like at a man whose virtues and vices can be discussed without fear

II

Winds

Winds! How can I know you?
Only your envoys speak about you
limbs of trees grasses bending under your palm
pointing here! here! Hardly have they done it
you are gone

Invisible you reign over the visible
the sudden banging of a window
hordes of clouds driven away
only wind chases another wind without hurting it
embracing tenderly they sow love death and destruction

O children of the winds—zephyrs with curly ringlets
playing on the radiant face of the south
tramontanes tradewinds mistrals—

Now there are only autumn blizzards
powerful gales mixed with rain
and gazing at Italian landscapes in photo albums

It Poured Stars

That August night it poured stars like glass
we made no wishes
but each star lit memories
like an explosion of magnesium that illuminates a picture

Hidden in darkness with his head raised
man recognizes the landscapes
that found a home in his skies
Only his eyes communicate
with the light spots of Libra
and the Big and Little Dipper
Arcturus shines with pink light
the North Star—our guide—
measures it with a grave look

In the silence experienced by generations
thought turns speechless caught suddenly
in the starry snare of eternity
helpless and pathetic at the same time

The Transfer of Power

This is the land of Sisley's trees flax candles of poplars extinguished
        among highways
and the trees of Pissarro potbellied apple and pear trees
in peasant orchards with the sharp green of grasses
Corot's hazels and aspens pale from dew and a mysterious light

It is also the land of Theodore Rousseau elms and hornbeams that
        speak no language
and try to be themselves nothing more not symbolizing anything
not expressing anyone's soul simply to be and to endure

Also Van Gogh's convulsive trees rejuvenated forests of Cézanne
and muscular limbs of Courbet
Watteau's groves lit through with mirrorlike happiness
the land of sweet France taken into art's loving captivity

O!

O, white flowers of shadow, the wild glistening of the river!

A Versifier Speaks of Painters

Perhaps painters were ahead of the poets
in their love of the world and their escape from the world
The joy of Matisse the discipline of Cézanne
Pissarro's peasant solidity and the madness of the Redhead
Miró's childish games between astronomy and a child's room
Arp's monsters under a calm indifferent sky among rocks on a beach
the lonely people in Hopper's American city
buffalo skulls on Georgia O'Keeffe's desert
the sublime boredom of geometry mystical attempts at monochrome
a point's infiniteness the rigors of Mondrian and Malevich
Francis Bacon's bloody visions between criminology and the last
        judgment
visions in turn humble and insane
free from words but awakening words of poets
ignoring the world and exploding the world
expressions of our knowledge and helplessness
conceived in a moment of inspiration and executed
with a craftsman's stubbornness
since in the end everything depends on endurance

Friends traveling companions
behind a wall separating us
I hear a brush thrown on the floor in anger
a canvas stabbed with the same tool that stabs the artist

I hear hours pregnant with silence

this pain and muteness last for weeks

until at last one morning a melodious whistle comes through the
    atelier window

lighthearted as a song of a blackbird or starling

praising the birth of a beautiful splash of green

Hearing the voice I summon scattered hopes

and reach for a piece of paper once again beginning

Anew

An Attempt

In a Brooklyn park next to plants and flowers
little signs with names written in Braille
for the blind

Try to close the eyes Try to imagine how it is
to know only the sign with an inscription
you catch a fragrance read the name with your hand
you must imagine the flower according to a name

Perhaps you are accompanied by a friend
who tells you about the flower:
I admire the accuracy of the description
shape size number of petals arrangement of the crown
height of the stem the leaf's form a perfect account

But a flower can be described only as a flower
Poets try to do this
also for those who look and do not see

There Are Poems

There are poems that are beautiful, and beautifully elaborated.

But we know poets who captivate us with totally unadorned yet noble speech, a nakedness that doesn't give the impression of nakedness.

So natural that it could stroll among people wearing coats without drawing attention to itself.

The nakedness of Mickiewicz. The nakedness of Dante.

Tombstone

They are saying good-bye.

Two women stretch out their hands.

A girl takes leave of her mother.

Next to them the father, lost in thought.

Here lies Aristilla, daughter of a rich merchant, loved by her parents. She died in Piraeus, 240 years before the birth of Christ.

On a neighboring stele another young woman extends her hand for an apple that a beloved young man is picking from a tree.

Nearby, a child clasping a dove.

Hermes is standing at the edge of the broken slab. He looks into darkness. Where the art of the sculptor doesn't reach.

Metope

Girls are leading a lamb in the sacrificial procession.
They are serious: they lead it to its death.

Behind, their companions carry pitchers of water and wine on their shoulders.

Young men, covering their faces with pleated tunics, lead a bull. With head raised it bellows pitifully.

At one side a soldier, seen in profile and leading a horse by the bridle, closes the procession. What is striking is the animal's nobility. Its eye. Its expression of concentration.

It Is Also This

Art casts a spell summoning life
so it can continue
but its space extends to the invisible
It is also an intelligence reconciling
discordant elements and similarities
It is brave
because it seeks immortality
by being—just like everything else—mortal

Safety

A Japanese boy, sitting on a leaf that hangs from a mulberry tree, is painting.

Why is it that no one shouts: "Hold on, you will fall!"

No one runs to save him.

It is the merit of the old, experienced artist. He has survived more than one earthquake, but he entrusts the boy to the mulberry leaf.

Equilibrium

A pink ear, transparent like alabaster. Folds and corridors along which the eye takes fright and is lost.

In the very middle, meeting rooms that pick up sounds from all the corners of the world.

Above the ear a tiny angel swings on a gray hair, with a band sealing its lips.

A Sentence

I depend on the sentence On a stop that seeks form
as orderly and modest as everyday speech
Everything in me awaits the moment when a shape
encloses the shapelessness where it was suspended
I suffer gently but persistently the pain of uncertainty
the dissolution of feelings and thoughts in which I live
as in a diluted space

It doesn't hinder me from admiring the linden branches
spread wide behind the window the screech of a magpie
annoying and blessed because it exists
it doesn't hinder me from taking in the heat
of this dry and tragic summer
But a sentence a reliable sentence
restores under my feet the firm earth

What to Do with Words

What to do with words
that have no object behind them
nothing to touch or taste
on which to rest the eyes
nothing to relate to human temperature

For example the word eternity
sterile pure cold as the glow of stars
leading us into a desert of interplanetary space
into diluted air the dead bottom of darkness
a word with no temptation no odor no color
a sound no tamed animal would obey
even the wind is more palpable than eternity
a huge number has at least an appearance of countability

But eternity? Once called up it rattles around the skull
once created it can't be erased from the dictionary
ownerless wild and monumental
one more proof of our madness

A Mistake

Huge canvases, on which ideally clean colors fill spaces precisely measured out with elegant geometry.

But in a corner of the room, the tender, delicate drawing of a leaf sketched with a quick masterly line, like a last fetish with which he didn't know how to part, like the trace of a farewell kiss to nature.

He shouldn't have shown it. The entire exhibition falls apart like a pile of cards, conscientiously executed homework.

Dear Goldberg

—Dear Goldberg play me one of those "Variations"—
Count Keyserling asked his musician
during illnesses and sleepless nights

Whoever knows the curse of insomnia
that has no relief
will understand Count Keyserling
who offered Goldberg for his art
a golden cup filled with louis d'or

Bach didn't hold it against him
because he obeyed the magnate's request
to make his music light and cheery
unwillingly

Styles

I look with sympathy at a certain poet of the middle generation. I always liked his poems, and looked for them in magazines.

I trusted his words and images.

Now he practices the grotesque, in poetry and prose.

Thus calm and gravity are no longer able to support the weight of our world.

The grotesque has sharp teeth and devours everything it touches, without sparing itself. It is a suicide mocking its own mourners.

The Poetry of Crumbs

He says whatever comes into his head. Pell-mell,
without rhyme or reason. The poetry of crumbs, peel-
ings, scraps, vague allusions, imprecise words, un-
finished thoughts. Exempt from beauty, allowed to be
sloppy.

The collective path of human myths abandoned in
order to browse the roadside grass. Here a clump
there a clump, together a thousand clumps next to
each other.

Looking at it in the future, they will wonder.

The longing for a lasting symbol. Not through
cracks, holes in fences, or cellars. To enter through
the front door, where the dead await the living with
matters of the utmost urgency. Where the living once
again become alive.

Whenever I Meet

Cherubim and Seraphim, these I can understand. But where do these fat crows in the garden come from, the branch bending under their weight?

I wonder at each sparrow jumping as if on a spring, I wonder at each wandering cat.

O secret, intermediate world, so you continue to exist?

Whenever I meet eye to eye with a dog standing on legs spread wide and staring at me expectantly and persistently, I can't resist the thought that it is for my abuses of speech, for my boasting and false tone, that he was punished by speechlessness.

III

Maurice

They call him names robber thief gangster swindler
street mongrel and brawler
He leaps onto the table interferes with meals
rummages among glasses and china
tears apart food parcels brings in his mouth a starling
that decided to visit the lawn in front of the house
and paid for the careless walk with his life

He demands categorically to be let in or out of a room or the kitchen
enters fierce battles with neighborhood cats
making the frightening screams of a predator in the jungle
He flatters no one is unyielding in his desires
indifferent to orders and caresses
yes caresses for despite his nature
they caress and cuddle him
enchanted by his soft lope and agile leaps
they give him the best morsels let him sleep on their beds

So love is not a reward for virtue and character
obedience or loyalty
but for charm and insubordination
for life itself in all its raw nakedness
Great indeed is our need to love

Under This Island

Under this island there is another island, maybe even more beautiful.

Smiling she swims toward it, uniting with a flash-like arc the rock, the air, and the water.

I would like to see you from all sides, creature, fragment, storm, splendid madness of a clear mind.

Funeral Stele

Here is the funeral stele of a female slave
whose beauty made her slavery lighter
A malicious barbarian damaged the tomb with an ax
chipped off the shapely nose the alluring lip
so only an outline of brow remains above the wound
two eyes staring intently at a mirror held in her hand

The beauty of this mutilated face moves us
while her frivolous gesture a hand holding a mirror
an attentive look at the reflection of her own face
bring Rome closer to us
than the severe profile of virtuous Aspasia

Tell Me Why This Hurry

The lindens are blossoming the lindens have lost their blossoms
and this flowery procession moves without any restraint
Where are you hurrying lilies of the valley jasmines
petunias lilacs irises roses and peonies
Mondays and Tuesdays Wednesdays and Fridays
nasturtiums and gladioli zinnias and lobelias
yarrow dill goldenrod and grasses
flowery Mays and Junes and Julys and Augusts
lakes of flowers seas of flowers meadows
holy fires of fern one-day grails
Tell me why this hurry where are you rushing
in a cherry blizzard a deluge of greenness
all with the wind racing in one direction only
crowns proud yesterday today fallen into sand
eternal desires passions mistresses of destruction

You Drown Me with Shouts

You drown me with shouts, laughter, the ringing of breaking glass.

Yet I call out with my hair standing on end, and my lips move like the lips of a terrified mute who at a banquet saw a wing of the conflagration flying toward them.

Ladies in a Coffeehouse

The ladies were drinking coffee.
They tore out my nails—one says.
The spotlight was turned straight into my eyes.
On me, water dripped for two days.
They ruptured my kidneys.
They shot my son, burned my father.
Ordinary Warsaw ladies.

Far Away

She ran faster than tears
ran straight ahead
no boundary was in front of her
no one chased her
no one was racing against her
luminous space waited
to take her in its embrace

Let the Light

Harpies, we are all harpies, my beautiful ladies. We give birth to children, we cushion the path for others, and we fill raised beaks with nourishing food.

Then we receive one or two blows to the heart.

We are resurrected. We remain with an empty interior where the husband's medals, scraps of shroud and diapers are lying about.

For others the bracing frosts of constellations, the sound of trumpets and flutes. For others a horse neighing in the darkness, the pathetic hoaxes of time, a salty breeze or a shout from the highest peak, the farewell salute of sailboats in fog and the monotonous ringing of buoys.

Let a she-eagle soar up, let the light, our younger sister, lift up the sacrifice of our boyish hopes.

Leave Me

Leave me in the uncertainty of sleep.

Submerged in warm breathing, in the shelter of the heart's slack rhythm and the butterfly flutter of blood. Leave me.

Because this is where I find in me the primeval valley of the Vistula, the green and radiant valley of Nineveh seen in enchantment.

The earth that I seek and recognize, to reconcile with it when it stands so motionless and eternal in the dusk.

Song

Why is this song gnawing at me today
a time to cry will come
The deep alto was with us for years
for years we ignored this song
carelessly we threw it to the winds
but it wandered over rocks and water
an echo repeats it and it sounds again
a time to cry will come

A Sigh

How I loved you things that are superfluous
boundless love friendship sacrifice virtues
met so rarely and paid for so dearly
how I cried over every betrayal every
disloyalty and every abuse

How I loved you things that are unnecessary
paintings words flowers and lovely faces
each blossoming meadow sunsets and dawns
how I loved you almost to excess
and how vexed I was you are superfluous

With Head Turned Away

When everything has passed, when I have enjoyed what delights me—that it is and that it lasts—I would like to be a statue looking at the sea, without a name, without an inscription, with my head turned away from everything that bores and torments.

To have darkness behind me, in front of me a bright sky, flickering lights on the water, and to feel on the stony face the southern sun.

Cry of Loneliness

Each wave shouts about it though it flows in a crowd of waves
each bird shouts about it though it flies in a great flock
wind shouts about it rubbing against grass and trees
only man is silent about it
only stone is silent about it

In the Street

Madwoman How easy it is to say
how easy to think
not the one locked up
but the one met in the street
seemingly similar to other passersby

How sharp becomes your eye
how quickly that flicker appears
the signal sensitive to every difference
—I've got you little one
A coquettish flower and wrinkled hat is enough
or a dangling old fur coat on a summer day
or when she talks to herself makes threats
the easiest one to recognize

But I think about the one whose glance is sharp as a knife
who squeezes tight fists in her pockets
I think about her whose own death is in her eyes
and the darkness she carries inside is her abyss
I think about the one who walks with eyes lowered
as if she didn't see anything ahead
stumbles and continues to walk

Before

"before he finished his first volume he was killed at the front in World War One"
"plagued by depression he committed suicide"
"during a visit to New York he unexpectedly died of alcohol poisoning"

—biographical notes in Stanisław Barańczak's
anthology *Love Is All That Exists*

But the one who reads your poems
doesn't care how much you paid for them
a pendulum is moving constantly from darkness to light
from light to darkness
How much nourishment can be found in madness
how much in an obsession with death
before they reach the crucial point
when nothing can be drawn from anything
when nothing leads to nothing
when nobody comes to the meeting

He Doesn't Know

He would sit in the corner of the room and give orders:
—Do this, do that, this way, that way.
He praised or blamed:
—It could be done better.
Now he is silent.
He doesn't know. He simply doesn't know.
How did it happen his certainty so suddenly turned into doubt?

Sharks

Be careful not to shed even a drop of blood. You will attract them.

Always hungry, they keep circling around you. Their shadows pass behind your windows. Suddenly they will appear from behind a street corner, they will break in, smashing the door of your home.

Ghosts

We were talking about ghosts. That some time they may appear before us.

They already called us on that misty, windy night —"Hamlet, Hamlet!"

We were wondering about poison. That one day we might have to drink it.

We drank it already.

We were thinking that the moment of trial will come.

Meanwhile the pilgrims we carried with us have been resting a long time at the bottom of the sea, and are no longer recognizable.

We think: starting tomorrow we will really live.

But this is already life, and some of us are dead for good.

Higher and Higher

Born on a trash heap, victims of seven plagues, we proclaim every day a victory.

One more day. I am still alive.

While the trash heap grows and lifts us up, toward immortality.

Demand It Courageously

Make some room for yourself, human animal.

Even a dog jostles about on his master's lap to improve his position. And when he needs space he runs forward, without paying attention to commands or calls.

If you didn't manage to receive freedom as a gift, demand it as courageously as bread and meat.

Make some room for yourself, human pride and dignity.

The Czech writer Hrabal said:

I have as much freedom as I take.

IV

Ash

As far away as the seashore you can hear
the song of a chain saw surely a funeral song
Hacked branches lie in grass with the crown of the venerable ash
until yesterday king of all the trees here
When you look closely at the cut limbs
it was clearly fated to die A brown damp patch
tells of a long and hopeless sickness

Skilled surgeons in green overalls
rest now sitting on the ground
under the bare stump of the operated tree
above them an empty space of air
still not used to the absence of branches
under the tree a dwarfed shadow ready to leave

Why

These wrinkles on the sun's face
this graying moon more misty at night
and the sacrifice of leaves by trees
still bravely shaking faded plumes
shining bodies of hornbeams shot by lightning black willows
in sickness in humiliation in injury of broken limbs
and this stubborn rain always appealing to us the same way:
Surrender   Why resist the inevitable

We Will Do It for You Nature

You abuse your power
earthquakes flooding rivers hurricanes
but I tell you a woodpecker's morning knock on a pine would be
      enough
resounding over the region as it hits right to the tree's heart

I know you are giving us a sign you live
that your power and anger still surge
at the bottom of oceans
You take revenge for your own wrongs
sneer at the stupidity of our trash heaps mock the poisoners
who tomorrow will fall victim to their own poison

You escape into the memory of your own beauty
look at your reflection in paintings by the masters
cry over yourself with polluted tears
your rapid breath heaves with the flame of burning forests

Despite everything it isn't hard to predict who will be the victor
you can lower your voice
we will do your dirty work for you

Everything to Measure

Oh no—paradise is not disheveled nature
bearded unkempt pines shrubbery branches
blue-black colonies of berries
looking out with the eyes of hunted deer
Paradise is a garden
where everything is to measure
joy but not wildness
not despair but melancholy
It is the victory of order

So what if on gravel paths
you sometimes hear approaching steps
above which a body had no time to take shape

Mavericks Heretics Spoilers

Though mavericks heretics spoilers
we are all children of nature
Just as a birth brought with it the forecast of death
so we wander among gardens
disinherited from wild meadows
greeting with our feet the roots of roots
the cradle of mortality

I Am Tired of the Omnipresence of Roses

A crowd of poets is roaming through the gardens
a plethora of stanzas about roses
roses tortured by love by admiration
My memory retains just two poets with flowers
Rimbaud next to a heliotrope
and Apollinaire with a colchicum

The Gift of Mediation

Shadow warns shadow that you approach,
light warns light.
Frightened, a wild dove starts up. You are an obstacle,
not foreseen here between the loftiness of pines
and penal divisions of low grasses.

You are a foundling looking for a family,
a prodigal son who has fled
and returns to bear witness to the independence
of trees and thistles, quick butterflies and dying dragonflies.

It is through them this moment of peace comes to us,
they help grace descend on the wing
of an unknown bird
and it is their voices—an ermine's cry, moan of a dove,
complaint of an owl—that remind us
the hardship of solitude is measured out equally.

A Quarrel about Experience

What does it mean: A Great Experience?

What does it mean: You have to go through it?

Through thirst in the desert? Frost at the North Pole? Cannibalism and hunger among fragments of an airplane crashed at the foot of the mountains? Suffocation from lack of oxygen?

The cry of a single steaming drop of water will tell you about it.

A single grain of burning sand.

It Comes Uninvited

That moment when reason understands it was cheated.

When inflicted harm appears in full clarity, and there is no justification for it.

When a writer throws the picture of his master from his desk.

When love and attachment realize they haven't met the trial of time.

When we remain alone, completely alone, with a chill in our heart.

But are we more unhappy than those who continue to stand by their old choice, only so they don't reject their past life?

I Asked

Was I a priest who didn't believe strongly enough?
A physician who neglected to perfect his knowledge?
A hermit who would slip away from his retreat?

Happy is a bird or an animal
with nothing to reproach himself

Not to Be Certain

The green of maple and chestnut leaves, seen against the sun, is transparent. The pond next to it seems almost black.

Through the dark, gluey surface of the water one can see moving shadows of huge carp with silvery red scales.

This is their promenade. They lead a quiet life here.

Unknown to them are the dangerous expeditions of migrating salmon, clear mountain water, the delighted leaps of trout. The park is the only region they know, their province, their paradise. They long for nothing else.

It is better to be careful, however, judging the happiness of others.

A Confession

—Don't call me as a witness. I won't be of any use.

I don't trust the testimony of my eyes, my thought loses its thread and, fearing the worst, doesn't dare reach the end. I do not know who I am.

What is the value of a being whose testimony is so frail and uncertain?

—Don't complain. For only you, among the different species, know the dignity of your weakness; and despite everything you labor to the bitter end against your own disbelief, ready to sacrifice your own frailty for an illusory brotherhood.

An Envoy

In night's coffin
in a grass basket
we floated carried toward unclear goals
Someone above marked us with a sign of fire of hunger
a deity of deities a good prince or lame old man

We floated without terror
the sea was bloody and mountains of dead
from the bottom swayed with a wave
turning the night sea into a cozy cradle

Filled with the secret knowledge of dreams
we were prey to symbols
crosses stars anachronistic animals
each of us had a split tongue
for simple and learned speech

—We are animals from blessed stables
whoever meets us let him run away with a cry
if other species still exist
in cosmic constellations from gentler myths

For You Europe

For you Europe we are a preserve of history
with our old-fashioned ideals
with our dusted-off treasures
with the songs we sing

Everything that is best we give away to be devoured
by the dragon of violence and sheer force
young boys beautiful girls
the finest minds most promising talents
offerings of flowers crosses words

Lighthearted heirs of solemnity
and promoters of hope
we are inheritors of a native rhetoric
that fits us perfectly—

though only yesterday
it seemed a bit too tight

Reading the Apostle Paul

The Lord dealt him blow for blow
blinding him with terrible light on the road to Damascus.
He began to spread a truth he persecuted till then,
from persecutor he became the persecuted.

Only once, faced with slander
and unjust suspicions of fellow believers
he recalled what he had suffered:
three storms at sea, shipwreck,
flogging, being stoned, several prisons,
and in a moment of exceptional openness
mentioned almost impersonally
his vision of a third heaven, adding:
—I don't know if it was for the living or for the dead.

It is this third heaven that makes one shiver the most.

Without Noticing

The sun lit up bright shrill insane
fleeing the onslaught of approaching clouds
it tried to tell us something with its shout
Someone strained his ear in suspense
someone else passed without noticing
The whole tragedy took place high above
where mortal hearing doesn't reach

Beautiful Sisters

No—memory is not alone
it has many sisters who are unlike each other
all hard working never resting

Their order must be respected
the oldest always continue to grow
while the youngest die before gaining strength and body
bringing successors to life

For nature doesn't rule the family of memory
it isn't an image even a reflection of an image
but a separate formation a presence apart
In the end we remember only the beginning
distant greenery before banishment from Eden

Rebuke

How clumsy you are memory
you lose everything that is most valuable
events words images

Memory madly striving toward the void
ravaged unfaithful memory
drowning the firm land of the past
deeper and deeper
destroying itself

Lawless memory you project
whatever you like on a screen
ignoring our expectations
Cunning one
you make false pacts with dreams
thoughtlessly confusing faces and gestures
turning those close to us into strangers
giving strangers unearned familiarity

Memory you work for us but never obey
you mock us when we look at fading photographs
at bereaved women
putting on again colorful dresses

Not Eternity and Not a Void

Time is in us and alongside us
but it isn't us
though the clatter of our heart
is also its clock

It is measured by our steps
but like the mythical messenger
light-footed Iris
always moves away from us with an unknown message

Someone might say
it stays close to us like a meticulous accountant
watching capital assets melt away
which willing or not
we must use to the end

Perhaps nothing in the world
is used with such wastefulness
or such stinginess
as time

But princes
ignoring their obligations
order it out of the way
Didn't Baudelaire say:
It is free time that made me great

Waiting for a Signal

From childhood to youth from youth to maturity
from maturity to old age—he wonders:
Why didn't anyone give me a signal
why was there no warning
no word of encouragement
I didn't know when my time is or who I am

If everyone around me was too busy
why wasn't there as promised
a guardian angel with shepherd's staff
standing by who would tell me at dawn:
Take heed this is the day you were waiting for
today you can do everything but not tomorrow
Maybe then I would soar up like an angel
and achieve the work that someone else
always does in my place

But friend—says the figure
with eyes the color of iron a face worn by years—
I haven't left you for a moment
I sang hymns at the appointed time
but your voice never joined mine

Orphaned

He doesn't even take out plates
he eats straight from paper on the table
with a fork with fingers whatever
provided it's faster

He would be repelled by his own messiness
if he weren't so indifferent
if she were still at his side
Rattling spoons she chatted
as life flowed through the room like a familiar river

In front of him a flickering TV screen
he doesn't notice
nearby a newspaper he doesn't read

But there must be a way

The Old Man

The old man fell in the mud and snow, got up, and apologized.

The old man forgot a bottle of syrup on the pharmacy counter, returned, and apologized.

The old man pushed his way onto a crowded tram, wheezing heavily.

The old man does not threaten anyone with his own death, doesn't share his despair with anyone, and doesn't complain that for him everything was at first too early, then too late.

The old man remembers he was put on a floe that drifted away, was thrown from the Tarpeian Rock, was abandoned in the desert, or starved to death in a pigsty. The old man's memory is the memory of mankind.

VI

Seated Woman

Wind wrinkles the pond's surface like pale skin
Do the weak love water? Do they seek resemblances in it?
Wrapped in a blanket though the autumn is mild
she doesn't even pretend to read
books have floated away like the plastic bag
carried over the pond imitating a swan
She sits with her face to the water
Happiness is to return
from behind hospital gates into the arms of the world

She sits with her face to the water
the green dress recalls the pond's murky pattern
on her head the bright tulip of a hat
its brim drooping as if wilted and discouraged
she spreads her hands contemplating her fingers
then quickly hides them from sight
On the shore enormous weedy leaves of burdocks
are like a carpet flying just above the ground
For a moment the sun adorns its chosen patch of water with bright
        colors
and the willows glisten

Before Dawn

For whom do they work so hard
what do they summon so stubbornly
repeating the same melody over and over
the same modest motif
sung with royal ardor

What in this asphalt suburb
could bring forth such joy
such exaltation of prayer when it is still dark
and not a single streak of light in the sky
betrays the approach of dawn

But they know somewhere far away
though not so far it can't be felt
spreading elm trees and thickets
of light green are full of movement
and brotherly chirping
gardens stand on tiptoe
watching for the procession of spring

They sense the heightened breathing of lilacs
childlike tears of hyacinths under the windows
O joyful and plaintive birds
why did you wake me with hope
while now I listen to you in despair
I can't respond to your singing
I only listen to you motionless in the darkness

Who Said

Who said that during the massacre of the innocents
flowers weren't in full bloom
the air breathing intoxicating fragrances
and birds reaching the heights of melodious song
young lovers entwined in the embrace of love

But would it have been right for a chronicler at the time
to describe these and not the street flooded with blood
screams of mothers infants snatched from their arms
thoughtless guffaws of soldiers excited by the touch
of women's bodies young breasts warm with milk

Burning torches rolled down stone steps
all thought of escape hopeless
as violence and terror gave way
to an even more horrible numbness of despair

At this moment covered in the southern night's shadow
a bearded man leaning on a cane
and a young woman cradling a child in her arms
were leaving the lands ruled by a cruel despot
carrying the hope of the world to a safe place
under silent stars where what was just happening
was inscribed for centuries

Speak to Us

Hesitant or self-confident? Searching or decided?
Doubting or arrogant?
Speak to us because we need to converse
Tell us we will respect the differences of others
carry out just laws

Speak to us because we were harassed by lies and violence
for too long humiliated and taught to be servile
for too long condemned to vindictive silence
Our relatives were deceitfully murdered
their graves trampled and a forest planted on them
in our dreams it grows like Birnam Wood
night birds weep in the branches
summoning us to rites of cleansing

Lord we aren't the only nation tormented this way
don't let us take pride in it

Yet We Desire It above All

Freedom does not mean happiness right away
the free world hides more traps than tyranny
mastiffs let loose from chains passions exceeding the horizon
steps entangled in the ropes of old bonds
that try to pull tight again

Freedom both for scoundrels and those
who sacrificed themselves for it
freedom for those who feel as pure as a diamond
and want to cut deeply surrendering passionately
to a new slavery—of hatred
from which the earth cracks like under dynamite
changing the course of rivers

VII

Lublin Elegy

So I was born on this patch of land.
What should I do to feel I belong here?

1.

She wakes in a convent boardinghouse
through the window a wide view over the region
It is morning
a Lublin morning
in a vast meadow nonmeadow among lush lindens
men and women go to work on a worn path taking shortcuts
they pass the Castle the space left from the synagogue
then the Orthodox church the open market

Lublin
not yet borderlands but already borderlands
embroidered cloths on tables holy pictures on walls
here Orthodox icons there Jesus with a flaming heart
pious chanting in different languages
mute air in which moans of the murdered are frozen
wailing thrust down a throat then silence
huge and final silence in the odor of choking smoke
and rags scattered by the wind

2.

In the cemetery mother father and sister
Mother alone near the Orthodox chapel apart
as she must have felt alone
leaving her native Moscow
its lights and loud boulevards

Nearby the grave of Czechowicz
buried among soldiers "fallen on the field of glory"
someone always brings flowers here
because the glory of his poems lasts and hasn't fallen
their sweetness disturbed by a prophetic vision of the future

He alone would know how to lament this city
who cast upon us the spell of its sleepy beauty
he would know how to celebrate the processions of phantoms
        lingering here
to find a prayer for *the burning of suffering souls*

3.

And I a small girl at the time
drinking in this dark busy world full of noise
and shouts in an incomprehensible tongue
that suddenly grew quiet on Friday evenings
when lights of the lit candles glimmered in windows
and in the thick dusk of Grodska and Szambelańska Streets an
       old-fashioned lamp
threw pale flickering gleams on leaning walls of houses

4.

Turn your eyes away from me gates of my city
city gates voracious gates
through which life departed from these dark passageways
O towers of my native city
you chased me across the world threatened me
I owe you nothing insensitive giants
who have survived without shedding a single tear
over the city of my childhood

Victoria

Why didn't I dance on the Champs-Élysées
when the crowd cheered the end of the war?
Why didn't I throw myself into the arms of a sailor
who walked down the gangway with a duffel on his arm
and ran toward me through the excited crowd
raging sounds of bebop
"*La Marseillaise*" and "God Save the Queen"
blaring from the loudspeakers?

Why didn't I break out a bottle of champagne
next to the two of them still dressed in English uniforms
not guessing one day I would stand at the end of their road?

Why was I fated to be on the main street of Lublin
watching regiments with red stars enter the city
crying with joy I would no longer hear the hated *Raus!* and *Halt!*
but torn by sadness this was the price for a lost dream
of a hero's triumphant entry on a white horse
for the return of those who twice cheated
didn't want to come back

So we stood—the ones who survived—
on the streets of Warsaw transformed into a desert
and today years later find ourselves
in the fading films of old newsreels
hard to recognize

Classmates

The Latin teacher's voice seemed a bit sharper
when she addressed them
(never by the first name).
Miriam was always perfectly prepared,
Reginka weaker but correct.
They kept together
and together left the classroom before Religion.

The last time we met unexpectedly
at the end of Lubartowska Street,
on the border of a freshly created ghetto.
They stood there timidly as if something shameful happened
        to them.

On the Road

The oldest trees
are in the Jewish cemetery

A crow
cantor struck speechless
does not sing

In a heavy autumn cloud
they pass by the thousands
over the treetops

You who are shut in the palaces of memorials
come out to meet them

through lashing rain
through lightning
you must go together

Those who don't have their own place
who are themselves fire and rain
unite now with you

Because it is not yet
the end of their end
it is not the end

A Procession

The dark forest of Dante
the forests of Shakespeare
are more true than the shadows of recollection

We glide
like sacrificial bulls with gilded horns
all our effort put into building the conviction
we won't surrender to sheer force

Blizzard hunger and exile
roll over us in a powerful wave
from underneath we emerge still alive
and see an unfinished landscape

The only deliverance is in keeping the rhythm
a vision of a harmony
that takes us like children into an embrace
innocent mother of consolation

Long Vigil

When will we return to the interrupted conversation?
Give me the place and address though the darkness is thick
and matches are wet from fog

I recognize footsteps
that approach and go away
how full the past is of images
cut through by sudden lightning

Streets and attics where we lived
places of deportation war humiliation and pain
—all drowned

Only sometimes when it's silent
a whisper can be heard:
we are here

It's two in the morning
why are you already having breakfast?

Separation

Men do not tell women about war
They are silent when a woman's hand touches their scars

What did *La Belle Rousse* know about the mud and blood
of the trenches in Champagne?
It's true Madeleine heard the artilleryman bragging
but this was only the beginning of Apollinaire's "little war"
it was still a clean job

Did Maria hear with her own ears about the life
of her beloved in Auschwitz?

Wasn't time too precious
to tell a young girl about a wound received in a tank at Falaise?

What woman was told about the hell at Monte Cassino?

But all of them wrote about it finally
to chase away night phantoms
not for the purpose of love

Why then do images of this and that other war keep coming
        back to me
from the letters of others from the poems
from the thirteen or more written stories

These tamed wars sleep in me
bringing back the ones I loved
who kept silent to the end

A Medium

To be everywhere almost at the same moment
without moving from a place
To look and at the same time
see other images deep inside

Pierre Bezukhov in a white hat
mingles among the soldiers before the battle at Borodino
the panorama of the army seen from a hill enchants him
glimmer of weapons and dark smoke rising from the battlefield

And right next to him Apollinaire who so lightheartedly
admired war's spectacle
—*how beautiful are the rockets lighting the night*—
before he found himself in the trenches and was struck by the odor
        of decomposing corpses
the curse of mud sickness of trench foot
before a splinter of shrapnel hit his head

And next to him singing Schubert's song about a linden tree
Hans Castorp hears the whistle of an approaching bullet and falls

These old wars though horrible
have a personality
people were still able to describe them
It seems as if I knew the First World War from close up
it keeps coming back to me through recollection
that others have preserved for me
For my last war there were no words left

Homage to Apollinaire

Unloved One *Mal Aimé* you ask us for the grace of memory
It is not the same as fame
you want love
because you weren't loved in your lifetime

May we never experience the pain of the abandoned
or orphans with false pride
You alone knew how to complain
so that your complaint became ours
we carried it together with you
on the streets in the midst of the blind crowd
and your voice was our voice
leading us in the footsteps of your fate

Because we needed one sharply outlined life
in the haze of so many others lived as if in a dream
though desires were strong
and outcomes seemed fixed in advance

To awaken—this is not given to everyone
As he moved he listened to the song inside
that made an alliance with the world
The bullet that struck his forehead in the trenches of Champagne
was like the star that chose him

VIII

A Small Girl Sleeps in a Stroller
at a Joan Miró Exhibition

She still sleeps but these games with form are for her
these puzzles with green squares
kites hanging in the sky and tamed suns
crumbs from a broken kaleidoscope
this fleeting fancy like a fairy tale
that now seeks shelter in her dream
from the crowd swollen as a river
filling the room

To Conquer the Mountain

To reach the summit
to conquer what is unconquerable
There are some who arrive at the peak
but think immediately of coming down
for no one can live on a summit

Hokusai tried to paint his mountain twenty times
How many times we will remember Cézanne
rejected by the *Salons*
embittered and unbearable
with the stubbornness of Prometheus
dressed in his worn-out frock coat
wrestling with Mont Sainte-Victoire
always defeated by it

For us today
he is like an unattainable mountain
constantly barring our way

"Give Me Your Hand, Darling . . ."

I like it when they walk holding hands
old or young
and you don't know or need to know
who is leading

On a square in the middle of Rome
he put his hands on our hands
resting on a railing

There was another hand
stretched out on a steep mountain
and the hands crossed on a *macebb'ha*
adorning an elder's grave

There was also
"give me your hand, darling"
the treacherous aria of Don Juan

A Manuscript

Through the glass of a display case
where Beethoven was born you can see a manuscript
with dozens of scrawls, corrections, and crossed-out words.
It is a letter to a powerful prince imploring him
to accept a symphony he has just composed.

No other composition by this genius
bears as many marks of exertion as this letter
to a ruler of a tiny state unknown today.

Meditation (on Czesław Miłosz)

We weren't worthy or sure enough of ourselves
to catch hold of the subjects beyond our reach
He must have known it if he encouraged simplicity
and warned against aiming too high even mocked it
But he warned in vain
because the very practice of art implies conceit

None of his young detractors outdid him
in the bad things he said about himself
He spoke courageously about faith
felt he was a Manichean but stayed faithful to orthodoxy
though doubts never left him
It was true—he admitted—he had a perverse mind
he was endowed more richly than others and he knew it

Sometimes he was hated for this
sometimes looked at grudgingly and rebuked
The half-educated would lecture him
there were those who tried with or without conviction
to move him to the bottom of the list
Like others he didn't avoid misdeeds
To be adored or rejected—
he chose the path himself
never in the middle

He compared himself to Job
but some who observed from the side
saw only favors of fate
as if he entered an alliance with the devil
for his fame embraced two continents
and he had a high place on the tower of poetry

He was only too aware
he didn't know and couldn't know
about what is the most important
he wanted to show the real and succeeded
but an impenetrable space
always hovered above this reality
as if a land of happiness was built over *Sheol*

Before his destined time arrived
he experienced the revelation of old age and slow extinction
Reluctantly and with delay the city
gave up its strongholds and ships

Farewell to a Bird

The stork with a broken wing
is no longer by the pond in the park
How did he perish? One could say heroically

When he felt his wing was almost healed
he soared suddenly into the air
looked down at the swans imprisoned in the pond
beat his wings in exhilaration
beat his wings desperately
and crashed into the water

Poor Icarus!
No one noticed his fall
not the farmer driving a tractor
nor the passengers in a red Toyota
busy passing a truck

Rehearsal with Toscanini

How they must have hated him
with his craving for perfection
when he interrupted them screaming louder and louder

He kept talking in Italian and forgot these were Americans
On the record you can hear his baton strike the stand
as if he trained circus horses with a rider's whip
Marcato! Marcato! and then *Piano! Piano!*
he sings as if he believes it will inspire them

He shouldn't have done it
because now a hoarse dry cough attacks him
he shouts *Falso! Falso!* meaning *Wrong! Wrong!*
and still shouts: *Andiamo!*

until the moment arrives
when we stop hearing him
The famous maestro disappears
suddenly merged with his orchestra

and the heavenly murmur of Debussy's "Clouds"
flows over the concert hall
envelops us all

Hilary Hahn

About to leave
he was stopped by a violin's unspeakable sweetness
coming from the radio
light and so tender that going away
would be robbing himself

He waited until the melody described a farewell arc
and performed in his place
a few interrupted steps

It seemed this was the end
he stood with his hat in hand and waited
but still it circled for a moment
as if dancing with eyes closed

Swinging the door shut
he heard only the name of the heavenly violinist

A Thank-You Note

Where does Vivaldi hurry
this red-haired Venetian priest?

He lopes with great bounds through the narrow streets of his
    enchanted city
falls in water up to his ankles on St. Mark's Square
flooded again by the sea

Where is Vivaldi hurrying
in "The Four Seasons" in his sonatas?

He hurries to be on time
running like a physician to save a patient
before the wild burst of stormy feeling
to which his music gives a harmonious answer

IX

Let's Not Sleep

Let's not sleep yet
as long as the gentle music plays
let's not sleep yet
as long as there is no sign of day
As long as we follow in night's steps
in brotherhood of darkness
let's not sleep yet
while the sounds forget time
let's not sleep yet
let's not sleep

How to Reach

How to reach this underworld—and is it necessary—
a labyrinth where you can make out
the thread wound by tired Ariadne
(you are Ariadne you will perish abandoned on the shore)

How to reach—and it is necessary—this underworld
of memory that sleeps and waits to be awakened
waits for grace of consent to what has happened
or perhaps humiliation from powerlessness
over the past

What was to be unity
lies like an overturned skyscraper on its side
filled with the echoes of pleas and farewells
of mirrors preserving the faces of the departed
To whom give a report? Where make an account?

Goodnight

Courageous is the one who falls asleep
and sinks into a country of deceit
You will be put to a trial
you can never win

You won't find a guide
who could call the shadows you meet by name
and the one you are looking for—won't be there

If names are mentioned
they will sound so incomprehensible
you will doubt your mind and your memory

But there is no escape from the violence
inflicted by the messengers of sleep

Over the Crisis

Don't lose the image—a voice warns
but it is the image that leaves me
more and more obliterated by the spreading light
of holy and accursed emptiness

And yet I hold you by the hand
The sun is high
and promises a long day
without any night without any night

A Message

Go to the park in the morning
before the sun's chariot rolls to the top
You will be alone
you will be a lord
among the crowned heads of poplars oaks pines

Go to the park in the morning in autumn
you will be ruler of the season
gentle as a caress
benevolent
between the terror of summer and winter

Go to the park on an autumn morning
It waits for you
its face hidden in shade

An Old Man Climbs the Stairs

Stopping in the stairwell to catch his breath
he turned to the window
a fragment of courtyard open trash bin
He looked a moment then began to climb

Just then two teenagers passed him
one lifting something heavy
to the old man it looked like a crowbar
Worried he squeezed the key in his pocket

Fugue

The shoemaker who repaired his shoes died
the tailor who sewed his clothes died
the physician who cured him died
the dentist who fixed his teeth died
his friends did an about-face
he stayed behind like an infant naked toothless disinherited

Nontime

To live through a week
to live through a year
through thirty then seventy years

But there were years no one counted
royal years
when we played under ancient oaks
and eternity was with us

Towers

A small Brooklyn boulevard over the East River
is called Promenade
it was a favorite spot to photograph the city's profile
with a sharp outline of Manhattan skyscrapers.

At lunchtime, benches turned to the water,
Brooklyn residents who worked nearby
sat with plastic sandwich boxes
and tourists with cameras recorded a view
duplicated a thousandfold on cheap postcards.

They go there now too
for though the two tallest towers have disappeared
the view still dazzles.

But where the two sister summits of the World Trade Center
        rose up
the eyes do not want to accept a void
and draw the familiar contours in the air.

The space between the towers is filled
by pale sky saved from the explosion,
underneath the constant movement of crushed elevators seems to
        continue
as hundreds of computers work silently,
transparent shadows pass from hand to hand
documents untouched by the fire,
and from telephones flow signals
that might be listened to in a million years
on an unknown planet.

I Saw

In a dream I saw those cities
San Francisco and New Orleans
then I saw them with my own eyes
But in my dreams the earlier landscapes keep returning
mocking what I learned and the four senses

Questions

What will we become
in what direction will we turn
who will judge us
who will reject us with relief
freeing us from the ties of art
which constantly demands something
asks questions
scorns an easy victory

Brodsky

The lagoon was witness to his winter days
to the harsh solitude he chose

The torments of attachment don't disappear
yet this evening of Venetian fog
and the pain of beauty are stronger than pain carried inside

How soothing can be distance from all the things
we came to love
the sad pride we can also exist here

A spot was waiting for him on the island of San Michele
even in exile
he was master of his place

He pointed out this cemetery
his love for the lagoon would be enough
to merit it

When the flatterers and slanderers fell silent
he heard in the bay the splash of a wave struck by an oar

Feeling the Way

The most beautiful is what is still unfinished
a sky filled with stars uncharted by astronomers
a sketch by Leonardo a song broken off from emotion
A pencil a brush suspended in the air

NOTES

9 **Evergreen:** The word "Evergreen" appears in English in the Polish text.

35 **Dear Goldberg:** J. T. Goldberg was the personal musician of Count Keyserling, Russian ambassador to the Court of the Elector of Saxony. Keyserling asked Bach to teach Goldberg some clavier pieces to cheer him up when he couldn't sleep.

93 **Our relatives:** A reference to the fifteen thousand Polish officers murdered in the Katyń Forest, near Smolensk, by the Soviet NKVD in 1940.

93 **Birnam Wood:** See *Macbeth*.

94 **Yet We Desire It above All:** This poem was written in the 1980s during the period of martial law.

97 **Lublin Elegy:** Julia Hartwig's mother was Russian and an Old Believer.

98 **the grave of Czechowicz:** Józef Czechowicz (1903–1939), a prominent avant-garde poet, was, like Julia Hartwig, a native of Lublin.

98 **"fallen on the field of glory":** A standard inscription on gravestones of soldiers killed in action. Czechowicz, a civilian, was killed by a German bomb in September 1939 on a street in Lublin.

98 *the burning of suffering souls:* A phrase frm Czechowicz's poem "A Pastoral Dream" ("Sen sielski") in his last volume, *A Human Note (Nuta człowiecza)*, 1939.

99 **voracious gates:** Reference to the transfer of Jews from the city to the nearby Nazi concentration camp of Majdanek.

100 **the two of them:** Two men with ties to Julia Hartwig who were soldiers during the Second World War. One was her future husband, Artur Międzyrzecki (1922–1996); he was in the Polish Army under General Anders, fought in Monte Cassino, and in 1945 found himself in Paris.

106 *La Belle Rousse:* Refers to Jacqueline Kolb, whom Apollinaire met while recovering from a wound at the front. They were married in May 1918; Apollinaire died six months later.

106 **Madeleine:** A young teacher in Marseilles whom Apollinaire met on a train. He addressed a vast amount of verse and correspondence to her.

106 **Maria:** The beloved and later wife of Tadeusz Borowski (1922–1951), author of the volume of stories about Auschwitz *This Way for the Gas, Ladies and Gentlemen.*

108 **Hans Castorp:** The protagonist of Thomas Mann's novel *The Magic Mountain.*

115 **macebb'ha:** In Hebrew *massebha*, a Jewish funeral stele.

ACKNOWLEDGMENTS

This project is supported in part by an award from the National Endowment for the Arts.

Grateful acknowledgment is made to the editors of the following publications in which these poems, sometimes in different versions, first appeared.

Agni: "A Sentence," "Everything to Measure," "Whenever I Meet"

Green Mountain Review: "I Will Perform This Miracle for You," "Return to My Childhood Home"

The Iowa Review: "Long Vigil," "Victoria"

The Manhattan Review: "A Manuscript," "A Medium," "A Procession," "Beautiful Sisters," "Far Away," "Ghosts," "Homage to Apollinaire," "Maurice," "To Conquer the Mountain," "Waiting for a Signal"

The Michigan Quarterly: "Classmates," "Lublin Elegy," "Meditation (on Czesław Miłosz)"

The New York Review of Books: "Old Fashions"

The New Yorker: "The Gift of Mediation," "Translating American Poets"

Poetry Daily (electronic): "A Manuscript," "Homage to Apollinaire"

Nominated for the Pushcart Prize: "Maurice"

A NOTE ABOUT THE AUTHOR

Born in 1921 in Lublin, Julia Hartwig belongs to the same generation of Polish poets as Zbigniew Herbert, Tadeusz Różewicz, and Wisława Szymborska. Her voice was shaped by the events of the Second World War and Solidarity, in which she played an active role. During World War II Hartwig belonged to the resistance movement as a runner for the Home Army while studying Polish literature at the underground Warsaw University; during the period of martial law, starting in 1986, she was a member of the Citizens Committee at the central office of Solidarity. Throughout the years of communism and after, Hartwig has been a liberal presence in Polish poetry. She has published more than a dozen collections in Polish, and her poetry has been translated into German, French, Italian, Greek, Lithuanian, Russian, Serbian, and English. The recipient of numerous awards for her work—among them the Thornton Wilder Prize, the Solidarity Prize, and the Georg Trakl Prize—she is also a well-known translator of American and French poetry into Polish. In addition to poetry, Hartwig has published book-length studies on Apollinaire and Gérard de Nerval. A member of the Polish PEN Club and an honorary member of the French PEN Club, she served three times as deputy president of the Association of Polish Writers.

During the years 1970–1974, Hartwig lived in the United States, first as a guest of the Iowa International Writing Program, then as a visiting professor at American universities, and again as a guest of the Department of State in 1979. Together with her husband, Artur Międzyrzecki, a well-known poet and prose writer, she published an anthology of American poetry, *The Modern Man I Sing*, that includes poems by Jeffers, Sandburg, Roethke, Wilbur, O'Hara, W. C. Williams, and others. She has also translated individual volumes by Robert Bly and Marianne Moore. Her prose work *American Diary* (1980) won the praise of Ryszard Kapuściński as a "model of travel reportage," and her recent anthology of American women poets, entitled *Wild Peaches*, was a best seller in Poland. A summa of Julia Hartwig's American experiences, her reflections on its landscape and history and its poets, found expression in the collection *American Poems*, published in Poland in 2002; many of those poems are included in the present volume.

Bogdana Carpenter is Professor of Slavic Languages and Literature and Professor of Comparative Literature at the University of Michigan. She is the author of *The Poetic Avant-Garde in Poland, 1918-1939*, and *Monumenta Polonica: The First Four Centuries of Polish Poetry*, as well as other works.

John Carpenter is a poet and literary critic. He is author of *Creating the World* and a study of the literature of the Second World War. Among translations the Carpenters have done as a team are seven volumes of poetry and prose by Zbigniew Herbert.

A NOTE ON THE TYPE

The text of this book was set in Kennerley, a typeface designed in 1911 by Frederic William Goudy (1865–1947). Commissioned by the publisher Mitchell Kennerley for a limited edition of an H. G. Wells short story, it became a very successful and much-used typeface. Kennerley was modeled after earlier Venetian faces, but its short ascenders and descenders are not typical of those types. The italic is almost upright and has a pen quality common to most of Goudy's italics.

Composed by Creative Graphics, Allentown, Pennsylvania
Printed by Thomson-Shore, Dexter, Michigan
Designed by Wesley Gott